PIVOT

IMANI MASON JORDAN

PIVOT

HELA PRESS
LONDON / WARSAW

FIRST EDITION

HELA PRESS
TEXT © 2025 IMANI MASON JORDAN
EDITOR'S NOTE © 2025 M.E. BAHRĪ

ISBN 978-1-917913-06-5
EDITED BY M.E. BAHRĪ
BOOK DESIGNED BY TEO SCHIFFERLI
PRINTED AND BOUND BY GRAFICHE VENEZIANE IN VENICE, ITALY

FOR A AND M AND J ALL WAYS

EDITOR'S NOTE
BY M.E. BAHRĪ

To engage with *PIVOT* is to work deep inside the current of a text that is already in motion. Less a composition than a convulsion, the poem is a turning of the world inside out. Imani Mason Jordan writes from within the long afterlife of colonial catastrophe, where language bears the memory of capture. Each word is a carrier of the weight of transit, across water, across empire, across forgotten architectures. Each word insists on its capacity to move, to transform, to pivot.

PIVOT is a book-length poem in four sections. It stands as an act of philosophical and linguistic marronage, a text that both remembers and reimagines revolution(s). It pivots between histories, between tongues, between wounds and their transfiguration. It turns language up and down, back and forth, against its own colonial architecture and makes of it something new: a site of metamorphosis, of rebellion, of sound. To pivot is to turn and to stay; to revolt is to rotate around a wound and name its origin. *PIVOT* carries the history of Haiti and the grief of the Atlantic. It turns language, like the body, toward possibility and in doing so, reminds us that every revolution is both descent and ascent, gravity and grace, and the break and the breath that follows. In its relentless motion, *PIVOT* reminds us that to write, to speak, to breathe in the wake of the Atlantic, is already to turn the world.

IMJ's writing belongs to a lineage of Black experimental poetics that recognises the page as a field of liberation as well as refusal. After the poets N. H. Pritchard and M. NourbeSe Philip, IMJ stretches syntax to its breaking point, testing the elasticity of the tongue, the English tongue(?), until it trembles with other frequencies. The text listens for the silences imposed by the archive, reassembling fragments of the unsayable into a grammar of haunting. IMJ understands rhythm as knowledge; that form is a sonic geography shaped by the Atlantic, by rupture, by return. Like the scholar Fred Moten, IMJ inhabits the blur between speech and sound, presence and absence, the word and its echo. But *PIVOT* is not derivative of these traditions, it is in conversation with them, a continuation of their insurgent refusal to let the tongue rest. Its organising verb, *to pivot*, holds a tension between motion and grounding: the dancer's continuous turn, that never seems to leave the floor, the revolutionary's movement that never abandons the people. In IMJ's hands, the pivot becomes a cosmological principle – the possibility of transformation within constraint, of rotation within captivity, of freedom that does not depend on flight alone.

The Haitian Revolution, and its continuous articulation of Black rebellion, undergirds the poem's architecture. It appears to be less as a reference than as vibration: a syntax of uprising, a grammar of revolt. The repetition of *throw, turn, pivot, undo, refuse,* becomes a litany of insurgency; echoing the recursive motion of revolution itself. The poem does not narrate the event but *performs* it, through the breaking of line, the mutiny of sense, the refusal of narrative containment. *PIVOT* withholds as a form of care; meaning becomes relational rather than extractive. In this, the poem participates in a decolonial aesthetics of *marronage*, the continual practice of escape and invention that Édouard Glissant described as *opacity*, a refusal to be made transparent to colonial understanding, the willingness to remain unexplained. To read *PIVOT* is to enter a zone where comprehension is not mastery but relation, where each turn of phrase asks the reader to dwell in uncertainty, to listen not decipher, where meaning is felt through resonance, rhythm and repetition.

The poem's language is both archive and incantation. It gathers debris from the colonial lexicon, idioms of *throwing, under the bus, out with the bathwater*, and reanimates them as ritual gestures, escaping their signifiers, undoing their banality. This repetition turns the idioms into sound, into pulse, into a kind of linguistic drumming. In doing so, IMJ transforms the detritus of English into an instrument of insurgent music. The task of the reader, then, is to hold and be held by the text's internal rhythm, to hear where it breathes and where it breaks, to make its form legible only insofar as it clarifies its motion. *PIVOT* demands ears over hands, an attunement to cadence, silence, and rupture, much as one attends to the body in motion.

ONE

men in linen fragments holding coin altar,
i write moulting, burning
heaving metamorphosis, symbol seeds,
the pivot smoulders
individuation by machete, to turn
return, not to same, circle, and broken
not disappearance, legibility spilling
downward in waterfalls, psyche ecology,
wound watershed, blood sap flesh vein,
pulse not spent

to throw something together, to throw
together, to throw light, free throw, unseat,
overcome, to dash, to abandon, to project, to
exert, to build throw, throw my weight
around, stone's throw, throw in the towel,
throw caution, throw doubt

throw money at something, throw money,
someone, throw under the bus, throw up,
throw out, throw away, throw some, maroon
cartographies, plantknowledge, map, drawing
steward turned sovereign, language the whip,
child wanders, collect coin, name fountain
altars, domestic revolution, writing indivisible
from turning sky, you watched mytheyes,
mouthed become, the bus, throw up, throw
out, throw away, in the throes of it, throw a
spanner, in the works, under the bus, down
gauntlet, the book, to the wolves

to the wind, abandon, and i was thrown,
build a language, language with rocks,
concrete glissant language, curl dash
down, the gauntlet, exerting free throw, hurl

grief cuts river in bone, i’m awake, stomach
pain, failed forms, shadow leaks
bureaucracy, marriage, mirror, memory,
chair leg, cutlery, one i perform, i repress,
i almost remember symbol,
symptom, linen shirt, no

no words, no vivid, no organ governs
exile, liminal airport hour, turning axis,
path, no spiral, down the gauntlet, exerting
free throw, hurl, in the throes of it, kick

kick rocks, persons who throw,
something projected, propel, propel
through air, rub, wear out, stone's throw,
the book, the game is, thrown as in lost,
intentionally, someone sabotage, the
game, often for money, throne, elevated
seat with back, intended for one person,
thrown, turning pages, turning toward,
turning tables, turning myth, psyche
curls the throat, somewhere beneath fire

something symphony dragged across what
language is, scaffolding, which gives us
light, which gives us calabash, gives leaves,
give bowl, ledgered things, unheld,
hovering, of noise, intention, history dream,
of ghost, maroons raising palisades,
outlawing outlaw poets, blood sap sweat
soil, charters, cane ripples syntax, forest
translation, spirit refuse, elevated seat with
back intended, for one person, throw a
spanner in the works, throw away, throw
caution, throw cold water, throw doubt,
throw eggs, in the towel, throw light,
throw money

at someone, something, throw
my weight around, throw out,
throw something together, throw the baby,
out with the bathwater, throw together
throw toys, to achieve, permanent
destruction, poetic form, lilt, roving
cattle, renegade swine, swine pirates,
cattle seamen, roving herds, rather rapid,
being what they are, they were freer than
they thought, freer then, rather rapid,
quite understandable, indigo rest,
sandwiched, slave pop, rather rapid,
quiet coffee, sugar quiet, the
exploitation of improper truths, the
evocation of slave, sandwiched

between her evocation, the baby out
with the bathwater, throw together throw
toys, out of the pram, throw under the
bus, throw up, thrown, thrown to the
dogs, to abandon, to build, to dash, to
exert, to fling, to hurl, to project, to rub,
wear out to throw, to throw cold water, to
throw eggs, to throw light, to throw my
weight, the truths of improper mortality,
venereal evocation, between pregnant

between infant, absurdities of food,
absurd moralities, seamen evocation,
maritime infant, sandwiched between
her evocation, tobacco morality

absurdities of quite understandable, cattle
pirates, renegade morality, seven hundred
and fifty great vessels, absurdities of risk, the
poetic form lilts, to achieve permanent
destruction, cattle swine, renegade
destruction, food for the negroes, improper
exploitation, declaring disease, proposing
improper, to throw eggs to throw light,
to throw my weight around, to throw
something, together to throw together, to
throw under the bus, to the wind, to the
wolves, to twist to turn, twist turn under,
under the bus, to unseat, to
overcome, writhe abandon

forsake, leave, desert arrival entrance,
emergence, landing assemble gather,
compile, construct babybathwater excess,
mistake, overreaction becoming
transformation, to breed hard animals,
morality when, evocation selfreproducing,
import, worked wild, captivity savage,
suddenly reproductive, reproducing self, the
one rule, between her evocation, the truths
of improper food, absolute dereliction,
words wild, worked too hard, cheaper than
to breed, forced to import, sandwiched
between her evocation, not pregnant,
venereal

to import, as in, supposition, analogy,
impact, assemble gather, compile, construct
babybathwater excess, mistake, overreaction
becoming transformation, unfolding,
emergence book record, chronicle, text break

fracture, snap, rupture build create, form,
construct cast toss, hurl, pitch cautionwind
recklessness, risk, impulse collapse crumble,
fall, disintegrate coldwater doubt, denial, you
ate tongue, dismissal concrete solid,
grounded, real construct assemble, fabricate,
design crack split, fissure, breach curl coil

bend, spiral dash, rush, sprint, scatter
sandwiched between, untamable tongue
africanborn, absent, every tract of forest, and
jungle, tongue suddenly

suddenly introduced, cheaper to buy,
minor functionaries, there was always a
minority, junglecame, denizens,
unnamable thighs, between genocide,
cruel aristocrats, the supposition of
analogy, sandwiched between thighs,
cheaper than to breed, to buy capacity,
sudden capability, on savages nervous,
absurdities of

absurdities of woman, minor function,
who bust nervous, continuous labour,
the few, one thousand negroes

majority achievement, the few absented, of
spirits burst, the many, whose only
achievement, which means, a minority of,
outlaw, soon every tract, the woods sought
outlaw, reproductive, the nervous, strain
functionaries, minor achievement, destitute
aristocrats, forced importafricans, analogy,
supposition, of pregnant women, of infant
morality, mortal labour, mortality population, minority
jungle, their bonds, their bonds,
over one thousand, fissure, breach curl coil,
bend, spiral dash rush

sprint

scatter

discard, throw away, dispose, reject

doubtlight, suspicionflicker, uncertainty,
edge, border, verge, brink eggstorm,
ridicule protest, eruption, erode, wear,
dissolve, diminish exert, apply, assert,
deploy expel, eject, force out, discharge
explode, burst, detonate, erupt exit,
departure, escape, leave
fight

battle, resist, confront fix, mend,
repair, manipulate flail, thrash, struggle,
flounder the negroes were worked too hard,
cheaper to buy than to breed, which means,
forty thousand each year, africanborn, the
supposition of analogy

which means negroes worked, cruel
aristocrats, destitute functionaries, refugees
of mountain, could accord to outlaw, foretold,
demeaned, the medium of conspiracy, the
contradiction of myths, the contradiction of
aristocrat, the aristocratic contradiction,
destitute myth, the negation of analogy,
resist, confront fix, mend, repair, manipulate
flail, thrash, struggle, flounder fling, toss,
chuck, pitch forsake, abandon, relinquish,
desert gauntlet, challenge, trial, ordeal
gesture, signal, motion, indication heave, lift,
hurl, haul hurl, throw

sling, lob implode

collapse inward, cave, contractimprovise,
invent, adlib, adapt kick, strikelash, protest
language, speechtongue, expression launch,
send, fire, initiate, lose, misplace, fail,
surrender, it was all quite understandable,
between her, forty thousand

minor functionaries,

unnamable spirits, the woods, the tract,
the forest, in the revolution of it all, the
principal origin of, the medium of,
contradiction, of conspiracy, the
monolithic cause, the slave rebellion, the
global, the revolution, the maroons
monolithic, the monolithic

themselves absented, existence foretold,
there was always, there was already,
tongue, expression launch, send, fire,
initiate lose, misplace, fail, surrender
moneyfire, bribe, payoff, corruption origin,
beginning, source, root outcast, exile,
reject, outsider outsider, strangerslave,
alien, foreigner outshine, surpass, eclipse,
overshadow overcome, conquer, prevail,
master overshadow, eclipse, dominate,
dim overthrow, topple, oust, depose power,
force, control, strength presence, being,
aura, proximity project, extend, monolithic

emit, cast, propel, drivepush, launch, rebuild, restore and, the few who succeeded then absented themselves, and majority minor, minor mountains, one three thousand, mountains foretold, structural merely, marronage, the scholars of the tradition, unnamable, the slave rebellion, abortive, uprising the slaves, slave armies, masters fearfully, expectantly, witness monolithic, functionary, destitute, the principal origin, termed medium, termed structural, the global situation, its structure, the slaves were merely, merely conspired, slave armies

forces, the slaves expectantly, the masters
merely, expectantly witness, obscure woods,
took to mountain, the border, accord,
demeaned, conspired, the slaves merely,
massive revolt, authority by revelation, by
revealing, morality, whose plan, the racial

arrogance, deceived to delay, abortive
arrogance, deflecting delay, attentive greed,
succeeded because, barren scholar, merely
passive, deflecting mask, deflecting night,
fascinated by, by the tradition, termed the
medium, because of its structure, the global
night, details of the ideals

expectant, fearful witness, deceived into
defeat, minor detail, into minor delay,
obscure movement, monolithic sap,
structural merely, expectantly, for a massive
revolt, project, extend, emit, cast tongues,
propel, drive, push, launch rebuild,
restore, reconstruct, repair rig, fix,
tamper, manipulate rockkick, resist,
reject, defy rocklanguage, speech,
structure, solidity rub, chafe, scrub,
erode, rupture, tearbreak, breach
sabotage, wreck, subvert, betray, scatter,
disperse, spread, shatter shadow,
silhouette, gloom, trace shatter

smash, break, splintersling, throw, hurl, fling
spanner, wrench, obstruction, disruption
spill, pour, overflow, scatter wild outlawry,
could accord their existence, the medium,
of lightning, of wind, and rain, and they
began, they began the mass, deflecting
their attention, they understood, abortive,
deceived, deflecting their attention, the
myths, the medium, fearfully, the slaves,
they understood, the abortive uprising,
deflecting their attention, of lightning, wind,
and rain, and they began, of lightning, they
began of wind, massive

obscure revolt, because of structure,
conspired sap, conspired wind, conspired
rain, expectantly, and then france, and then
again, again britain, and then spain, the racial
arrogance, deceived into delay, greed
masked, detailed, the medium of conspiracy,
of wind, and rain, they began, no monolithic
cause, no monolithic passive, merely global,
but this is not to say, the mass destruction of
the objects, the details of the night, the
rebellion spread, the global situation, the
slave rebellion, the racial arrogance, the
colonials had deceived details of wind,
deceived rebellion

hurl, fling spanner, wrench, obstruction,
disruption spill, pour, overflow, scatter
spotlight, highlight, expose, illuminate split,
divide, break, cleave throwaway, disposable,
expendable, fleeting throwback, echo, relic,
return throwdown, challenge, clash,
confrontation throwout, discard, remove,
eject throwup, vomit, purge, expel throes,
agonystruggle, spasm throne, seat, rule,
power, throwncast, discarded, disoriented
thrownagain, repeated, reborn,
rethrown through, across

beyond amid toypram, tantrum, one hundred
thousand angry blacks, the revolution, quickly
the rebellion, who conspired, who tongue
alone swept, its centuryold vestiges, its
promised obscurity, its rewards, propitious
for them, betrayed it, betrayed me, they
began lightning, they heard wind, they
suddenly betrayed it, their treason,
insurgents shortlived, expectantly tongues,
propitious, their treason, succeeded
because, slave armies, whose plan,
fascinated by wind, by rain, their promised
reward, reward not forthcoming,
insurgents rejoin, and

betray it again, massive revolt, transformed
into black armies, transformed into rebellion,
transformed into betrayal, transformed,
spread, alone had swept the plain clean, had
vestiges of slavery, centuries old, had
toward, had hatred, had knit the movement
back together again, had suddenly, it
seemed, military, wounded again, before
joining, the mass destruction of objects, the
racial arrogance, from that moment on, the
evolution and, the abortive uprising of
slaves, the massive revolt, the
grand historical parade, the first overall

seduction, the black revolution, the
movement back together again, the abortive
uprising of slaves, deflecting their attention,
greed masked, bloody, thrownagain,
repeated i'm here, i'm here to seduce you,
reborn, rethrown through, across, beyond,
amid toypram, amid tantrum, give up yield,
outburstprotest, toss, throw, fling, pitch
towel, surrender, turn rotate, pivot twist,
twistcoil, distort, contort, departure

undermine, weaken, subvert, sabotage
underthrow, fail, fall short, misfire, undertow,
good, by callout, underbus, betrayal

scapegoatsacrifice

pull, drag, current undoing,
unravelling, collapse, downfall, unseat
dethrone, displace, voice remove, speak
of rain, of lightning, of wind, of exslave

the slave whose military genius, whose old
intimacy, whose very attentive mystery,
who mysterious achievements of men,
burned ears, whispered name, black
armies, had swept the plain clean, futile
comparison, fertile plain clean, futile,
furtive glance, mysterious, burned ears,
unsurpassed, stormy ideologue, the larger
suppression, propitious for them, marching,
barren, much

grander presences, wounded by treacherous
betrayal, wounded by old intimacy,
wounded by legend and existence,
wounded by academics, by scholars, born
into them, still classic, still
strangulation, diplomatic, conspiring to
deny, haiti burned the ears, whispered its
name, mouthed become, their properties,
the mass destruction of objects, old
vestiges, intimacies the first,
the first commander, the midnight
administration, the still classic ridicule,
the weaponry of strangulation,
anticipated, and excelled, the records are
there, undoing, unraveling, collapsed

downfall unseat, dethrone, displace, remove
voice, speak, utter, express, vomit, expel,
purge, throw up, upweight, upburden,
upmass, pressure wear, erode, fade,
exhaust wind, breeze, twist, momentum
wolves, threatpredators, judgment writhe,
squirm, twist, contort cast, toss, hurl, pitch,
curl, coil, bend, spiral, dash, rush, sprint,
scatter, exert, apply, assert, deploy, fling,
toss, chuck, pitch, hurl, throw, sling, the
child wanders, collects coins, names
fountains altar, domestic revolution, writing
indivisible from saintdomingue, from
turning sky

you watched mytheyed, you mouthed

becoming, grief cuts rivers in bone, i am
awake, stomach pain, failed forms, the
shadow leaks bureaucracy, the
weaponry was ridicule, the revolutionary
heights, irresistible new world, that was
born in them, no one could have guessed,
the burning of moscow, the struggle
against bonaparte, who drove out the
memory, marriage, mirror, their
academics, conspiring to deny, no one could
have guessed, where anticipated, mysterious
men fill the histories, the records, the island
for selfheroism, no doubt

with due anonymity, foe sacrifice, no doubt
with witnesses, the records are there, no
doubt she gave signal, the unsurpassed
study, their ideologies, their heavytongued
achievements, they had shown their
capacity, their promised reward not
forthcoming, apply, assert, deploy fling,
toss, chuckpitch, hurl, throw, sling, lob,
kickstrike, lash, protest, project, extend,
emit, cast, propeldrive, push, launch, rub,
chafescrub, erode, sling, throw, hurl,
fling, toss, throw, fling, pitch, turn, rotate,
pivot,

twist, twist, coil, distort, contort, writhe,
squirm, twist, contort, exert, apply, assert,
deploy, throw baby out, withbathwater,
discard the revolt, fade very attentive,
legend, at the beginning of power, furtive,
futile conspiring, futile beginning,
its very existence, they had shown
their capacity, second to no fighters,
in any place or time, for
independence,
individuation by machete, the records are
there, the reason simple, in the larger
suppression of the fact, the mysterious
station, with much grander presences,
no hesitations, no monoliths, back together
again, the burning, anticipated

excelled, non doubt, with due anonymity,
non doubt, with diplomatic strangulation,
the fact, their weaponry was ridicule, their
weaponry was born in them, the reason
simple, they could not maintain, without
independence, theyliberty, without
independence, they place, or time, slave
army wounded, no one could have
guessed

guessed the power that was born in
them, the economic organisation, the
international diplomacy, the global
situation, no revolutionary heights, no
grand presence, deploy, throw out,
bathwater

essentialexpendable, discard, throw in the
towel, surrender, give up, throw
cautionwind, act without fear, abandon
caution, throw light, on reveal, on clarify,
on throw, down the gauntlet, challenge,
throw up, vomit, expel, throw under the
bus, betray sacrifice, throw money, spend
without think, throw faded, amongst
descendants, second to none, any place,
and the reason was simple, becoming
aware of oneself as a people, the clever
lucky illegitimate scatter, the
disparate rapids, factory essence

crucial continuous, no body of similar
states, no blood, with its language, no
readymade complete, propagandistic
miracles, mirror, memory, marriage,
chair leg, cutlery, the one i perform, one
i repress, i almost remember symbol,
symptom, linen shirt, no words, vivid,
organ governs exile, liminal airport hour,
turning axis, not path, not spiral, turning
pages, turning toward, turning tables,
turning myth, the psyche curls the
throat, somewhere beneath fire,
something symphony dragged across what
language is, betray, sacrifice, throw money

something, spend without thinking, throw
 my weight around, assert dominance,
throw rocks, kick rocks, protest, express
frustration, throw toys out of the pram,
have a tantrum, overreact, throw the
game, sabotage, lose intentionally, throw
together, create hastily, improvisation,
thrown to the dogs, abandoned, left to
fate, left, thrown away, discard, dispose
 of, throw back, left return, recall
scaffolding, which gives us light, which
gives us calabash, gives leaves, give
bowl, ledgered things, unheld, hovering,
of noise intention, history dream, of
ghost

maroon raising palisade, outlawing outlaw

poets, blood sap sweat soil, charters, cane
ripples syntax, forest translation, spirit
refuse, fate, throw away, discard, dispose
of, throw back, return, recall, throw up,
expel, puke, throw from hand, send
away, with force, throneseat, power, of
leadership, of rule, throwing stones,
judging, criticising, thrown together,
created by chance, chaotic unity, thrown
from throne, overthrown, lost power,
stone's throw, short distance, closeness,
oh the throes of it, struggling, in a state,
painmen, in linen fragments

holding coin altar, no, no vicious flourish
society, innumerable streams, mountain
island, ranges coalescing, rivers unusual,
like tropics, no lusciousness variety,
natural exuberance, violation property,
rights, vigour, cruel tortures, continually
enclosed no, factory dwelling, more
impetuous than the torrents, they will
arrive everywhere, flourish on the brutal
exploitation of palm, cane talks a few feet
above banana, trees rounded, leafless,
pear clusters, giant umbrellas, enclosed
the factory, with vigour, low and
continually, behold, crowning continuous

no rippled the breeze, dwellinghouses,
huge feathers, sixty no seventy feet, huge
branches, field upon field, coalescing into
rivers, the devastation of continent, the
lightnings raise trophies, the
courageous chief only, the throes of it,
struggling, in a state of pain or effort, to
the wolves, to be exposed, to danger or
judgment, to the edge, pushed to limits,
near breaking, point throne, fragile,
fleeting nature, sutured escape, you call
for change, windmomentum, for change,
undertow, subtlestrong

subtlestrong pull, rupture, influence,
breakdown, division, grouped distance, a
few feet above, sunbaked, waiting traveller,
slave and slave justice, dwelling sea-like,
unclouded, tropicalvisible, continuous
soothing murmur, leafless column,
undertow, subtle yet influence, pull,
breakdown, deep rupture, shatterdivision,
shatterdestruction, breaking apart, edge,
borderline, on the verge, for collapse

for falling apart, disintegration, crackdivision,
small break, leading to something,
largerspanner, spanner in

the works, obstacle, disruption,
sabotage, destruction, ruin, crack crown,
imperfection authority, or rule, expanse,
and filation, glissant, pageclosed, open
word, glissant, while groups,
undergrowth, and precious, luxuriant
abrupt, precipitous invectives, more
impetuous than the torrents, everywhere clr
james, looked clusters, murmurs, branches,
the slopes of hills, abrupt jacobin
mountains, covered to summits, mango,
orange trees, a mass of red golden
fruit, arid green leaves, huge feathers

scrupulous, everywhere clr james,
i write moulting, burning, healing metamorphosis,
symbol seeds, the pivot smoulders,
filiation place, open dictate, decree glissant,
decree james, fracture tremor, realignment
collapse, flux, turning point, transition,
topple reorientation, vortex, black burnt
bright blank gleam, shine ash, bleak dark,
ink mass, send, dismiss, drift driven,
mass of snow, mass of leaves, due course,
current drive, slipglide, slide edge, garment,
individuation machete

turn, to return, to same not, becoming circle,
and broken is not disappearance, is not
legibility, spilling downward, in waterfalls,
in psyche ecology, wound up, as
watershed, blood flesh, sap flesh, veins, this
pulse not spent, current drive, slip, glide,
slide the edge, of garment to feel, to
perceive,

sense sentiment, sensual sentient, nether
below to tread to rub, to turn to load, to
wheel to shake, to shiver heavyweight, to
tear, peel or perform, to enjoy chewed
over, my dear, my stronghold city,
persevere ground, preserve this soil

black earth, painstaking, maroon
application with cartographies,
plantknowledge, map, drawing steward
turned sovereign, language is the whip,
the child wanders, collects coins, names
fountains altars, domestic revolution,
writing indivisible, from saintdomingue,

from turning sky, you watched with
mytheyes, mouthing becoming grief, cuts
rivers in bone, i am awake, stomach pain,
failed forms, the shadow leaks, marriage,
mirror, memory maroons, raising
palisades, outlawing outlaw poets, blood
sap sweat soil, cane ripple

spirit refusal charter, syntax forest ledger,
persevere this ground, this soil preserve
black earth, painstaking application with
zeal, clip clasp, lump log, block country,
country club, nightclub, bookclub,
comedyclub, supperclub, breakfastclub,
socialclub, lunchclub, fightclub, boysclub,
girlsclub, chessclub, golfclub, healthclub,
yachtclub

clubsandwich, clubsoda clubscene
clubmusic, join the club, club together, clip
clasp, lump log, block country, country club,
nightclub, bookclub, she would have
welcomed the nomenclature, under the
auspices of a simmering volcano, the
poverty of blood, its language

ceaseless battering from disputation, no body
of similar type, a simmering volcano, under
auspices, misery, and vice, of foreign pens,
and the gulf that separates, where she was
born, the original home, nightclub,
bookclub, only the frame, only ancestry,
the other end of the curve, club together,
further thousands, by no means
unintelligent, ending in upheaval, from
island to island, landstanding, to evils,
proposals reactionary, sympathy with late,
with slow, with discovered, plantation
labourer moved to language, life under
its wing, the coloured missile, countryclub

clubmentality, clubutterances, the supreme
wrong of goodclub measure, the
rudimentary conditions of the gap
constantly growing, the entire clubisland,
entire upheaval, the salvation of
manufacture, the antagonism of races, the
racial arrogance, rudimentary qualifications,
scholars of note, from without, from
within antagonism, by expressing
sympathy, not scorn, as such the very
conditions, the life of household
necessities, the blue of condition, civilised
agitation, black mass constantly
growing, lifelanguage, used by the hour

every hour, all variations, still lives,
irresistible naked, anxious to be
assimilated into language, into black
masses, into food, clothing, household
necessities over large areas, still lives, the
capital city, the propulsion, in any other
part of the world, crux orbit pulley, adjust
gear axle, reposition knot move, step
spring bounce, toggle joint link, glide
turntable crank swash reverse navigate
spinout circulate evolve, adapt recalibrate
torsion, gimbal coil revolution, spiral
compass gyre, gyroscope modulate
realign, bushing flux reel, transition
crossroads pole

axis swivel, hinge, rotate, turn rotate,
central core, spin hub, balance shift, pin
fulcrum, circle orb, point twist, motion
direction, reorient loop, bearing focus,
wheel swirl, perch crux, orbit pulley,
adjust gear, axle, reposition, knot move,
step flinched, and moved to
language, agitations, quantities of
civilisation, pens, paper, bicycles, plates,
pots, without but from within, not knees,
not cloth, buses, elementary, clubscene,
clubmusic, join the club, club together
clubcard, clubmentality, she was clubbed

T

W

O

the revolt fades, very attentive, legend, at
the beginning of power, futile conspiring,
futile beginning, its very existence, they
had shown their capacity, second to no
fighters, in any place or time, for
independence, individuation by machete,
the records are there, the reason simple,
in the larger suppression of the fact,
the mysterious station, with much
grander presences, no hesitations, no
monoliths, back together again

which gives us light, which gives us
calabash, ghost, upheaval
calibrate verge contour, hinging
counterweight, overturning, sudden
end, apocalypse, i'm unveiling,
overthrow pivot, axis catastrophe, crisis
upend, rupture, a child wanders,
collects coins, names scattered series
with its rapidly transported blood, with
its language, its soil, within which its
sap still runs, a local type, hue, frame,
and scaffolding, organ governs exile,
turning tables, turning myth, beneath
dragged

which gives us light, which gives
us calabash, ghost, upheaval
outlawing outlaw poets, she
would have welcomed the
nomenclature, the ceaseless
battering from disputation
auspices, misery, and vice, and
the gulf that separates, the
other end of the curve, cyclone
mutiny undoing tilt, undoing
pivot

not knees, not cloth, buses, elementary
utterances of the supreme wrong of
good measure, the salvation of
manufacture, the antagonism of races,
conflagration

crescendo escape sympathy with late,
with slow, with discovered, plantation
labourer, moved to language,
agitations, quantities of civilisation,
pens, paper, bicycles, platepots,
the burning, anticipated, and excelled,
no doubt with due anonymity, no doubt
with diplomatic strangulation

old french, to turn, or from the racial
arrogance, the rudimentary qualifications,
scholars of note, from without,
from within the antagonism of
conditions, the civilised agitation, the
black masses constantly growing, the
life of the language to be used, the hour,
every hour, all beleaguered, beguiled, so
curt, itself, removed from slavery, the
contrast between rudimentary
conditions, pin, possibly from old french

pivot, to turn, or from vulgar latin root

pipare, to chirp

suggesting movement or turning, figurative
use, pivotal moment, developed in the
century, semantic blood, their own
humankind, to forks, paper, pencils, cloth,
the continuous conditions, agitators of the
lost horizon, the black massed
conspicuous capital, they live, in any other
part of the world

with blood, and brilliance, with boldness, to each of these distant infants an assortment of letters, distinct infants, longing eyes, itching feet, irremediable poverty, incensed vanities made clear, not confided, like revelations as obscure truths, obvious truths, the time had come to finish, sprout wings, she declared, is need be, the usual accompaniments of struggle, of grief, the rudimentary accoutrements, to fight, and die for, to be assimilated into revolution, rose to call, passionate islands against warring

the great bulk of people wanted no more,
bloodshed, the only revolt, hard animals,
morality wild, captivity the one rule,
between her evocation, the truths
imperialist powers, untoward, mass
intervention, slave armies, against
warring diplomatic, conspiring to deny,
haiti burned the ears, unnamable thighs,
between genocide, cruel aristocrats, the
supposition of analogy, to buy capacity,
sudden capability, on mountain, against
forest, gains plantation,

settled communities of escape

escaping africans,

blood sap flesh veins, the limits of agony,
the injections of poisonous precipitations,
stretched medicines,

patient poisonings,

passion unspent, the mimicry of grey,
outstanding auburn, men in linen fragments,
molting, burning, symbol seeds, smoulders
individuation, individuation by machete,
circle, not disseverance, not disappearance,
legibility spilling downwards, cartographic
knowledge, steward language, whip
language, writ indivisible

savages nervous, absurdities of woman,
minor function, who bust nervous,
continuous labour, the few, one thousand
negroes, no one could have guessed,
anticipated, mirror function,

gives bowl, absolute dereliction, words
wild, worked too hard, venereal, to
import, as in, supposition, jungle
suddenly introduced, cheaper minor
functionaries,

there, grinning stockades, exacting skulls, ceaseless,
hardbaked earth, tropical earth, the sun, rude
contrivance, earth cords, skull grin, bestial,
tropical contrivance, intelligent resentments,
pliant whalebone, grinning ceaseless,
stockades exacting, tropical earth,
intelligence, supple, and pliant, impertinent
follies, jawsick, bestial, ceaseless, grinning,
rude contrivance, whalebone cord, betrayal,
wounded by old intimacy, wounded by
legend, and existence, wounded by
academics, and by scholars, born into
them, still classic, still strangulation,

mysterious men that fill histories, the
record, the island for selfsacrifice, no
doubt with no doubt, with witnesses,
the records are there, no doubt such
impertinent follies, jawsick, elliptical,
ruptural poetics, nonlinear, lyrical brutalism
language, haunted grammar, disjunctive
mother wound, mother tongue, libidinal
fragment, minimal,

expressible, sublimity book, these shards
exilic, photographic, scant libidinal, and
thanatocratic, continuous labour, the few,
one thousand negroes, majority
achievement, the few, absented, of spirits
burst, the many, whose only achievement,
which means, a minority of, outlaw, soon

every tract, the woods sought outlaw,
reproductive, the nervous, strain
functionaries, minor achievement, destitute
aristocrats, forcedimportafricans, analogy,
supposition, of pregnant women, of infant
morality, mortal labour, mortality population,
minority jungle

jungle, toussaint learned to draw,
jawsickness, impertinent practice, latent
smattering, crushed, frighted, this
intelligence, which refused the elements of
education, women, of infant morality,
mortal labour, mortality population,

aristocrat, the aristocratic contradiction of
destitute myth, the supposition of analogy,
this intelligence, which refused the stockades
of grinning skulls, this intelligence, which
exacting, and pliant, this tropical whalebone,
this jawsickness, it was, it was medicinal,
circumstances conspired, for her integrity,
bestial, supposition, of pregnant women,
cruel aristocrat, destitute functionary,
his forty thousand minor

his minor functionaries, unnamable spirits,
refused the woods

pulled arms around bullets, the finality,
political direction, surveillance reigns borders

borders harden, when the tower fell i walked out
barefoot, arriving late, you taught me how to listen
for archetype, for monolithic cause, it
all leaks bureaucracy, poetic

form lilt, roving cattle, quiet coffee,
improper truths, the principal origin of
the medium circumstance, livestock, jawsick,
lawlike, ridden impertinent, these latent
smatterings, this intelligence, which
refused, those who profit by advantage,
those when exception, medicinal, unusual
intelligence, steward of all livestock,
circumstances conspired, by suicide, or
bands of free men, the

fastness of mountains, fortified ditches,
to cultivate remarkable herbs, unusual
coachman, her taste, the master conspired
circumstance, the circumference of men,
maroons, the circumference of mountains,
intolerable, and refused,

refused absurdities of morality,
seamen evocation, maritime infant, tobacco
morality, the cattle pirates, absurdities of
risk, the poetic form, the principal origin
of, the medium of

the africanborn, it was all quite
understandable, between his forty
thousand minor functionaries, mother
wound, mother tongue, the boldness to
evade, reproduced to prayer, the orator,

the prayer, the orator,
contradiction, to draw, smattering
knowledges, this intelligence, and
resentments, pliant like whalebone,
exacting, law, slave justice, the boldness to
prayer, unusual livestock, exploitation,
declaring disease, proposing justice

justice indivisible, the most fitted lightnings,
onehanded to announce thunder,
onehanded from fearless, onehanded from
accident, fortitude violation, onehanded
spirit preserve, make use, medicinal, her
unusual intelligence, her fortitude of spirit,
invectives against disease, invectives
against torrent, everywhere indelible traces,
who for on bent backs bore whole
structures, whole saint domingue society,
whole resentment, everywhere people,
impetuous traces of disease, just jawsick,
elliptical, ruptural poetics,

mackandal vigour, toussaint learned also
to draw, most fitted, vigour, cruel midst, of
property, the hand of the slave, the hand

hand of nonlinear, brutalism language,
lyrical haunted grammar, disjunctive
mother wound, in tongues, contradiction,
of conspiracy, the monolithic cause,
the slave rebellion, the global, the
revolution, the maroons monolithic,
the monolithic themselves, absented,
their existence foretold, there was always,
there was already bent

backs, onehanded from fearless, no
monoliths, back together again, the
burning, anticipated, and excelled,
no doubt with due anonymity, no doubt
with diplomatic strangulation, nondoubt,
the fact, their weaponry was, their weaponry
was born in them, the reason simple, they could

not maintain, without independence, they liberty

refused bold spirit, everywhere
the indelible whalebone, the hero, the
rights of the human trophy contingent,
vigour continent, cruel tortures,
continually enclosed, factory dwelling,
more impetuous than the torrents, they will
arrive, dwelling like a sea, unclouded
tropical

wont preservation, all of them did not
submit, all of them with ditches, with
palisades, fortified fastness, reestablished
in her honour, her fortitude of spirit, her
onehanded honour, mackandal the orator,
mackandal the invective, mackandal the
courageous, the fearless onehanded
continent, absented, their existence
foretold, there was always, there was
already, to achieve permanent destruction

herds, rather rapid, being what they are,
they were freer, freer then, rather rapid,
quite rest, slave pop, rather sugar
mackandal the orator, the island of
mountain ranges, the natural exuberance,
unusual lusciousness, different only in
superior strength and, her beauty, cruel
torture, rippled five, footleaves, dwelling
houses like sea, crowing feet

structural everywhere people, impetuous
traces of just disease, just oration,
remarkable herbs,
circumference of men, of maroons, the
circumference of mountains,
honour, toussaint medicinal, her unusual
intelligence, rather rapid, quite coffee,
one three thousand, mountains foretold

invectives against everywhere indelible
traces, who for on bent structures,
impetuous traces termed structural, the
global situation, its structure, merely, merely
conspired, armies forces, the slaves
expectantly, the masters merely,
expectantly witness, obscure woods,
vigour fortitude, indelible,
bold lightnings announce, brutal honour,

devastation trophies, breeze, of
dwellinghouses, of huge feathers, the
slopes of hills, solitary roves, a mass of
green leaves, mountainsides,
everywhere, vicious flourish, unusual
lusciousness, tropic exuberance, plan, the

racialarrogance

deceived to delay, abortive arrogance,
deflecting delay, attentive greed, succeeded
because, barren scholar, merely passive,
deflecting mask, deflecting night,

mountain islands, ranges coalescing, rivers
unusual, like tropics, her unusual luscious
variety, undergrowth, and precious,
luxuriant, abrupt, precipitous invectives,
more impetuous than everywhere,
like clusters, murmurs, branches, wild outlawry,
could accord their existence,

lightning flourish on the brutal
exploitation of palm, canes talk few feet
above banana, giant umbrellas,
enclosed the factory, low, and
continually, crowning continuous, rippled
the breeze, dwellinghouses

only grouped distance, few feet above sun,
baked waiting, continually unloaded, waved
the five, footpalm, one, handed crowning
distance, rippled cane

lusciousness, tropic exuberance, arid
red, abrupt fruit, tidy coffeetrees,
conspired sap, conspired wind, conspired
rain, expectantly, and then france, and
then again, and then britain, spain, the
racial arrogance, deceived into delay,
greed masked, detailed, the

medium where she, throve on this
devastation, brutal millions thrived, crowning
perfectly, on the sloped of hills, ferocity,
which surrounded, habitual, licentious child,
irascibility, mountain range, courageous
trees, solitary or in groves, rose on the
slopes of hills, the abrupt, and precipitous
summits, indulgence, degradation, which
surrounded the child on every side, a
sea, no monolithic cause, no monolithic
passive, roving

merely global, but this is not to say, the mass

the mass destruction of objects, the details
of the night, the rebellion spread, the global
situation, the slave rebellion, the racial
arrogance, the colonials had deceived, the
where she, in the conceit of isolation, the
irreverence of degeneracy, the turgid,
overheated society, the insolent, elegant
prejudice, the boredom of abundance, sixty
tidy coffeetrees, dice, and black women,
contrivance, nameless rude energy, like huge
feathered feet, abundant leisure, ledger
seeking overcome, those nameless men,

dice, and black women, irreverence,
overcome, always visible in the unclouded
tropical air, always visible in the rippled
soothing murmur, always visible in the
precipitous undergrowth, the wild boredom,
food, drink, dice, black women, work is
work, is an island of mountain, revolutionary
peasants, extermination, spite prohibition,
our god who rouses waves, our god who
rules storm, she watches us, thick black
volumes, smoke in tongues, flame leaping,
destroying salvation, tirelessly seeking,
most obvious, because they have suffered,

colonials had deceived, the details of wind,
the rebellion, one hundred thousand angry
blacks, the revolution, quickly the rebellion,
who conspired, who alone swept, its
century, old vestiges, its promised
obscurity, its rewards, propitious for them,
betrayed it, betrayed me, they began
lightning, they heard wind, they suddenly
betrayed it, their treason, insurgents short
in the unhealthiness of a climate, the
indulgence of every wish, the open
licentiousness, swallow tongue
the foundation of colonies, the
irreverence, and turgid, nameless
insolence, every wish added to the open,
vicious society, coalescing into rivers of
lusciousness

this page is left intentionally blank

THREE

the forests at night, the signs of unrest, revolutionary tracts, murders, and mutilations, bloodily, repression, for and against literature, circulating, running for their lives, perish violent interruptions, testifying magnitude, declamation, argument, abuse, applause, interests presumed, the depths of passion aroused, of dissent or approbation, this prestige, their influence, bent backs, who bore submit, who bold intolerable, refused spirit, vigour fortitude, indelible, and pliant, everywhere the indelible, the hero, the rights of the human race, trophy continent, courageous bent backs, bold spirit chief, lightnings announce, brutal honour, devastation trophies, wanted to preserve, wont to preserve, all of them did not submit, all of them with ditches, with palisades, fortified fastness, she decided that old life was over, she decided a new one begun

to achieve permanent destruction, poetic
form lilt, roving cattle, renegade swine,
swine pirates, cattle seamen, roving herds,
rather rapid, necessity, gangs of hundreds
on huge sugarfactories, a thoroughly
prepared, and organised mass movement,
after voodoo incantations, and the sucking
of blood, torn flesh, redhot pincers, slow
roasted on fires, incessant guerrilla warfare,
revolting slaves, condemned expensiveness

a carpenter between boards, meek,
prospered, chaos insurrection, a hundred
thousand revolting slaves, jean francois,
biassou, l'overture, hunting down the
recalcitrant, treacherous solution, the black
revolution in san domingo, field upon field,
the light green sugarcane, the fivefoot
leaves of banana trees, crowing perfectly
leafless columns,

waiting for the parched, and sunbaked
traveller, small, scrupulous coffeetrees,
abrupt summits, luxuriant hardwood,
unscrupulous intrigues, vested interest,
against wealth, against reason, the

managers, and stewards, the radical propagandists, their strength in the masses, a fewhalf, hearted attempts, everybody conspired to forget, since when, turgid, overheated society, since when did property ever listen, the unhealthiness of the climate, the habitual ferocity of parents, the degradation of human life, open

licentiousness, abundant leisure, the rude
energy of nameless men, irreverence, and
degeneracy, the insolence, the storming,
alarming, and envy, seventytwo thousand
masters, four hundred thousand enslaved,
import britishsold, to french, increasing
colonial produce, seeming eternal, the
score of humanity, more resentful, to
abolish trade, intractable, more ready for
rebellion, twothirds africanborn, more,
more ready than creole

unscrupulous intrigues, vested interest,
against wealth, against reason, the managers,
and stewards, the radical propagandists, their
strength was in the masses, a fewhalf, hearted
attempts, everybody conspired to forget,
since when did property ever listen, at first,
then again, and again, made it ashamed of
itself, made it leaders in terror, prosepoetry,
and flowers, so flagrant a breach, your glory,
your liberty, hour after hour, when property,
listen, the propagandists were helpless, the
few who openly opposed, more resentful,
more intractable, they tired their fortunes, they
tried fortress france, airing themselves, torn by
inner, and outer contradictions, thenceforth,
prosperous possession, having no enemy to
fight, one, and indivisible, they created

the slaves, revolutionary peasants, worked
the land, aimed at extermination, in spite of
all prohibitions, boukman, our god calls
upon us to do good works, boukman, to
revenge our wrongs, cecile, who rouses the
waves, and rules the storm, she watches
us, each slavegang, burning plantations to
the ground, rose thick black volumes,
smoke, which came in tongues, flame
swallowed leaping, in tongues destroying
tirelessly, tongues seeking salvation most
obvious, because they have suffered much

unobtrusive entrance, so wantonly, so
ferocious, she decided that old life was
over, she decided a new one begun,
revolted slaves, unobtrusive, perpetuating
resented injustice, secret communication,
men of bitter education, nameless men, she
decided, on guard against moment, on
guard against planter, the slightest material
interest, her own wife, and two children, her
own momentary passion, the revenges of
property, surprisingly

moderate, returned in kind, at the slightest provocation, these plantations stood their lot, our god calls good works, which speaks in the hearts of us all, throw away the symbol, she sees all the white man does, revolutionary peasants everywhere, voodoo conspiracy, rites, and talk, since the revolution, the extermination of oppressors

quite understandable, indigo rest,
sandwiched, the revenges of property
surprisingly moderate, returned in kind at
the slightest provocation, these
plantations stood their lot, our god calls
good works, boukman, which speaks in
the hearts of us all, fatima, throw away the
symbol, she sees all the white man does,
dutty, revolutionary peasants everywhere,
voodoo boukman, conspiracy, cecile, rites,
and talk, since the revolution, the
extermination of oppressors

the forests at night, the signs of unrest,
revolutionary tracts, murders, and
mutilations, bloodily, repression, for and
against, literature was circulating, running
for their lives, perish violent interruptions,
testifying magnitude, declamation,
argument, abuse, applause, interests
presumed, the depths of passion aroused, of

dissent or approbation, this prestige, their influence, bent backs, who bore submit, who bold intolerable, refused spirit, vigour fortitude, indelible, and pliant, everywhere slave pop, rather rapid, quite coffee, sugar, quite the exploitation, improper truths, the evocation of slave, sandwiched between evocation, venereal evocation, between pregnant, between infant, the truths of

improper mortality, absurdities of food,
absurdities of morality, seamen evocation,
maritime infant, sandwiched between her
evocation, tobacco morality, the absurdities

absurdities of quite understandable, the cattle
pirates, renegade morality, seven hundred,
and fifty great vessels, absurdities of risk, the
poetic reestablished in her honour, the
numbers lilt, swine, and cattle, lilting poetic,
i think i need to take this more seriously,
lilting, no way to separate, no way to dull
ache, to fragments, i think i need to take
this more seriously, the forests at night, the
signs of unrest, revolutionary tracts,
murders, and mutilations, bloodily,
repression, for, and against literature was
circulating, running for their lives, perish

violent interruptions, testifying magnitude, declamation, argument, abuse, applause, lilting, no way to separate, no way to dull ache, to fragments, again established, her honour, her evocation, reorganised in her fortitude of spirit, her onehanded honour, we have soup, everyone is always sorry after forgetting, the food comes before the cigarette, the ceramic bowl, the knife, this one has rhythm, this one can't help, mackandal the orator, mackandal the invective, mackandal the courageous, fearless continent, that, which does not, the unsaying of everything, possibly neither, and failing at both, this being a writer, and being a woman, this failure of becoming, so i don't smoke it, i turn back, a plant moved roughly, for fifteen minutes we orchestrate the kitchen, declaring of its seriousness, toussaint, boukman, mackandal, i write the language of ships, lilted numbers, one thousand five hundred eight seven ships, i write the language of hypocrisy, my longterm condition, too hard to breed, this language of absurdity, this trade language, i order soup, not selfreproducing

no monolithic cause, principal origin, i eat
mimic, for cowardice paid heavy, several
degrees of enthusiastic agency, attention
turning, lady best, been tears, between the
18th and 20th arrondissements, between

marseille, and bourdeux, a list of numbers,
hover page, graphic ledger, numerical
concrete, maritime bourgeoisie, their
clashing interest, in paris a man sits in the
corner, eating my order, eating soup, the
waiter who is also

the chef, i don't remember, because
commitment to being a writer or to being a
woman, because mimic, bird mimic, soup
mimic, table knife, bowl, and plant pot, i'm
sitting at the table writing, ordering

i try to write san domingo, i try, i don't understand, i don't understand how to write a book, i land in paris, i land in marseille, i land a symphony of bowls, i mispronounce soup, don't get me started, the man eats my order

don't get me started, as if i had a right to be
here, and she leaps, she leaps for the father,
raging deities, stranger soil, the africanslave
disrupted from familiar earth, labour
expropriated, society abandoned, in exile
from traditions, letters of blood, and fire, i
remember, the numbers scroll, hover
numbers, to carry soup, this particular breath,
banal trees, beneath curtain, beneath
scaffolding, banal trees, pretending not to be
blown, several paper layers of soup, there is
desire, there is distance, fragment fatigue,
the dull ache of

analysis, the persistent almost, i think i need to take this, their maritime friction, tobacco teeth, take this more seriously, the forests at night, something that goes with what i have, in the book i climb a hill, the hill is named after my mother, i am serious, i am serious about being a writer, in the dream about being a woman, a black woman, i eat mimic, for cowardice paid heavy, several degrees of enthusiastic agency, attention turning, lady best, been tears, between the th, and th, between marseille, and bourdeux, a list of numbers, hover page

graphic ledger, numerical concrete, maritime
bourgeoisie, their clashing interest, i am the
song singing the unsaying of everything,
empty room drinking, drinking wine, don't

get me started, a plant moved roughly, a
ceramic bowl, a chair, a knife, because my
condition is long term, i mimic the sound like
a bird, before it was mine, i orchestrate the
kitchen, seven hundred great vessels, bonds
burst, and running, unable maroon spirit, i
mimic like a bird, i build a language of
absurdity, glissant, been tears, between
18th, the 19th, between marseille

between bourdeux, fanon, rocks, and
continuous frame, no monolithic language,
wynter, voodoo artists, I want blood
language, cesaire, the cane processed
immediately or it rots, a list of numbers,
hover page, graphic ledger, numerical
concrete, maritime bourgeoisie, their
clashing interest, in paris a man sits eating
soup, some say they played no role, even
the cloth is imported, flammable betrayal,
rebellion strategy, the mountain where my
mother speaks, a modern life from the start,
three hands worth of artists, my long term
condition, in the hour

between whatever counts as the morning,
and whatever still smells like meat, like
tobacco, this hot year, i sit down to write
history, trembling architecture, mimicked
movements of the table, tobacco mouth,
delayed betrayals, delayed meat, more like
motion, resentment or terror, blood
language, the sap was flesh, i write san
domingo, i try again, i scratch out revolution,
and write sap, i wrote arteries, i wrote you,
because it has always been, the pressure of
invisible empires sleeping beside my bed,
my always dream, mutilated bananas, wet

stone terrace, cassava, calabash, abandoned
mudslicked bones, roving herds of renegade
seams, stolen pigs, just the fact of them, the
fact of return, flesh reorganising refusal, the
limits of agony, jawsick, saltheavy, leaden
skinsick, brutal revenge flame or the clumsy
dignity, this is what language is, something
dragged across the floor, ledger, like,
spectral above my writing, structures more
intimate, forest, sap, knife, spoon, ship, echo,
free than they might be, a black woman
dream, dice, and black women, her master,
her zombie mimic

her mimic wife, in dreams, i'm always
arriving late, always without luggage, a rage
barely spoken, circular, spiral, broken, the
transcendent function, the sky offers only
half of anything, always naked or bleeding
or politely explaining my delay, linen shirt
who said nothing, and pointed out nothing,
but existed vividly, mountains, plateaux,
forest, jungle, savannah, all spilling into the
highest waterfalls, blood, sap, flesh, veins,
arteries, his pulse not spent, torn, twisted,
stretched beyond form, supple whalebone, i
dream in fragments, i wake

with soil beds for fingernails, the whip is
language, the self before it is broken, they
return to the body, they fortify their forest
fastnesses, i have to take this more seriously,
medicinal plants, revenge, which in the
psyche means balance, obedient repression,
what is repressed must return, delayed,
cautious, eventual, the symbols, the burning
house, the mountain trail, the outstretched
hand, even history becomes a dream, a
dream the world forgot, jung, kairotic
time, chaos mountain, the unconscious,
and the consciousconverging myth, leaks

leaks the everyday, in the personal, the personal is turning as in metamorphosis, as in self, as in fate, psychic maritime, orientation individuation, individuation as machete, spiral life, rupture choreography, cosmic, rage barely spoken, circular, spiral, broken, the transcendent function, the sky offers only half of anything

the sky offers boukman, offers fatima,
brings erzulie's mirrors, how many
seats, how many years, the duties of
cecile, and erzulie, the black madonna,
black woman, i must take this writing
more seriously, neither the oldest nor
the most constant, the restricted
geographical areas, the chronological
sample, one can be certain, only one,
among all the mutations, that, which
began the fundamental arrangements,
the human cost, the human cutdown, a
given social

configuration in the same rare species, a
given status for the group, of walls
separated by pure and impure, impure
liquids, impure sperm, impure blood,
impure creation, impure flow, stanched
impure, impure liquid, his history is a
record of crises, and conscience, his history
a record of origin, neither heavenly

nor earthly, neither mortal nor immortal, on
the edge of hunger, and immiseration,
agrarian, stranded outside, where you would
rather be, wretched, the everexpanding
global archipelago turning, as in
metamorphosis, as in self, as in fate, the plot
of psychic maritime orientation, the spiral
life by machete, rupture choreography,
cosmic, a rage barely spoken,
indistinguishable from the collective, the
long unraveling of saint domingue, like the
turning of a clock etched, the land by
blood, and salt, and mango trees

i write to you now not in grief, but
in becoming, hoping your hands still trace
the margins of my dreams, where symbols
spiral like seeds, and the revolutions still
dream, i've left, not in bitterness, but
in the knowledge that some structures
collapsed, you taught me how to
listen for the archetypes, not just the
death of masks, beneath ache, the
burning, and blinking, the wildfire edge
of edges, surveillance reigns, borders
harden, the light striking false illusions,
off, off, the neoliberal dream, the romance
of control, the house built with someone i
loved, when the tower fell i walked out
barefoot, arriving late

alienating assimilating concomitant paralysing result, independent political action impossible, thrust dialectics, scandalous impasse, virulently good, the great silence, and beautiful and virulently legitimate, rhythms of poetic discourse, epistemology, cesaire the poet, the quid proprium of things, forest phenomena, permanent below revolution, halfstarved, bewilderedly

FOUR

dismantled new, generations of african
leaders sustain, institutions
critical and new, society cannot be built without
them, consecrated life to the defence of the
blacks, excoriated imperialism, placed
black labourers at the centre of world
events, black workers, all who labour
colonial, turn cheap wage, or market, driven
peasants, slave revolts, strikes, millenarian

movements, masses, guard your liveries,
guard parchments, fastidious tiles, who
drags her misery from court to court,
assisted in her magnificence, her
malevolence, permit sublime, my hand in
yours, profaned, sullied, the game is thrown

intentionally someone sabotages the game
often for money throw toys out of the pram
to throw rocks kick rocks, throne, elevated
seat with a back intended for one person, to
throw cold water, thrown to the dogs,
someone called to build a language,
lawlike, with rocks, concrete language, and i
was thrown to thanatocratic wisdom, lawlike
thanatocratic, thanatocratic logic, agrarian
thanatocratic, thanatocratic ledger,
legacy thanatocratic, thanatocratic,
necropolitical maim, temporal necropolitic,
libidinal necropolitic,

necropolitical infrastructure, analysis,
biostability, opaque necrophilia,
thanatocratic abjection, investments, the
right, the right to aftershock, libidinal
thanatocratic, economy, optimismdeath,
world elliptical ruptural poetics, nonlinear,
lyrical brutalism language, haunted
grammar, disjunctive mother wound, mother
tongue, libidinal

fragment, minimal, expressible, sublimity
book, these shards exilic,
photographic, scant libidinal thanatocratic, i
vacillate, flint, grovel, the literature in me,
the language, ignominious,
innumerable metaphors, libations,

strident, syncopated, to pivot as in to twist to
turn to hurl to fling propel to writhe to curl
as in persons who throw something as in,
throw the baby out with the bathwater, as
in propel through air, throw eggs, thrown,
to rub, wear out

shaking, the sky was wide, giving
nothing, no plantation eternal,
individuation by machete, turning as
in metamorphosis, as in pivot, as in
fated maritime orientation, spiral life, as in
rupture choreography, cosmic rage,
circular, barely spoken, the transcendent
sky offers only half of anything, in
dreams, i'm always arriving late, always
without, naked or bleeding or politely
explaining my delay, linen shirt, who said
nothing, and pointed out nothing,

but existed vividly in mountains, in forest

plateaux, savannah, all spilling into the highest waterfalls, spitting blood, sap, flesh, veins, arteries, torn, twisted, stretched beyond form, supple whalebone pulse, or the capacity to hold contradiction, transformation fragmentation, something must break the island embers, dreamsight, the ruins, something is being born, of walls separated by pure, and impure, and impure liquids, impure sperm, impure blood, impure creation, impure flow, stanched impure, impure liquid, her history is a record of crises of conscience, a record of

origin, neither heavenly nor earthly, the
bottommost place, nadir, the rung, hitherto
no name, brief hiatus, wretched, local terrain,
cutdown, the same rare species, felicitous
eruption, performative place, the seduced,
and harshly intensified, repressed
sanitisation, lawlike, vigorous, discursive
institutional, elaboration, the secularising
heresy of laymen, the group, of walls
separated by pure, and impure, the religious

intellectual laywomen, janusfaced, epochal
redescription, enactment, transomed, to take
one from another

another reoccupying, degodded, and either mortal or immortal, on the edge of hunger, and immiseration, intrigues home to roost, but after the troubles were over, these bastard proclamations, they seemed to go mad, a body of pretty applause, very patient, and forbearing, agrarian, stranded outside, wretched, the ever expanding global archipelago, neither the oldest nor the most constant, conciliatory seas, approbation, the object of solitude, the equilibrium of broken, political treachery, at the anointed time, and place, at this dangerous

moment, give proof your repentance, the
insurrections show strategy, and tactics,
show oneness of origin, revolted fogs, the
interview ended amicable, produced, and
reproduced, a systematic pattern, their
usual disregard, maroon imitation, the
interview ended amicable like, the slave
even as property, the ceremony of great
reconciliation, loud applause, as stipulated,
the petty desire for domination, loving play,
and loose living, their usual, scarlet healed
wound, ringing call for battle, their passions
insidious, groaned under iron, until
provision,

baggage recruit, the common standard, a frenzy of excitations, a rage revolution, everything before property, before frightful atrocities, the inoculated arrival, imposing ceremony, mendacious, coffeedrenched, with the blood of their own humankind, incarcerated, to win they had almost to destroy the island, the great bulk of people wanted no more bloodshed, the only successful, that very devastation, famine frightened, hopeless repeated shocks, an unalterable decision, most extreme, the wild hordes of black coffee, drenched

with the blood of their own human, her heart
sank at the prospect, political treachery, this
dangerous moment, the most extreme, forged
by circumstance of war, and barbarism
achieved, young slaves divinely inspired,

eclipsed, and armed only with stones,
charged bayonets, picks, and hoes, and
sticks, armed with language, clutched horses,
pulled off riders, they put mouth around
canon, died in alpine prison, the great bulk
revolt, pulled bullets out of arms, swarmed
over guns, and gunners, silencing nothing,
two thousand lay dead upon the field,

awaiting restoration, awaiting order, nothing could stop devotion, revolutionary association, temporary equality, broken things, impudent soldiers, lying frayed, and nerves, exhausted dishonesty, the most sincere attachment bound master to slave, these men who had become our children, neither locks not bolts, on our doors, the opprobrium, and dishonour in which they lived, enter a villain, idyllic, the destruction, and convulsion of despair, we live in peace, in pretensions of vanity, let slip the elegant drapery, disgusted

interruptions, won't express, masterly
disapproval, celebrated speech, still
clamouring peasants, the harsh obediency
of parents, property they would not touch,
whatever the status of its mother, these
elegant phrase makers, these astute,
eloquent, assiduous rioters, coffeedrenched
to envelop the enemy, seeking to crush him
by weight, these preliminary manoeuvres,
landing, and split, they quarrelled, tearing up
all of france to suppress the black revolt, the
only successful ocean, oceans obscuring
origins, neither ship nor atlantic

nor saint domingue, o my body, dim,
deceiving echo, its narrow church, simple
moral outrage, emptily, the labours line of
vision, i am writing, notes toward an
investigation of libidinal self, saint
domingue, san domingo so that i might
seek myself, how problematic, how crass,
to find myself in starving haiti,
dispossessed lands, the dispossessed
self, how grotesque, how empty, these
gestures, these solidities, cultural
representations, the primacy of class,
pivot, pivot, imagined past, very real, but
what of now, what autonomous

struggles of race, and gender, starving haiti,
conventionalised affective, libidinal
operation, starving sudan, logic, the regular
details demonstrating, starving congo, the
dispossessed lands, the dispossessed self,
how grotesque, how empty, these gestures
of solidarity, the cultural primacy of class,
these representations, the affective
conviction, demonstrating particular libidinal,
always economy, necessarily transindividual,
always lipid affective logic,
conventionalised affective, lipid operation,
the

regular details demonstrating affective conviction, demonstrating a particular libidinal economy, always necessarily transindividual, the libidinal economy of mass, black mass, a fundamental vector of group identification, pushpull cohesion, political fantasy, not everyone dreams the same dream, irregularity of sorts, abstained fantasies, that being said, primary unmediated form, the black madonna, erzulie, what dreams of ours are projected upon a real land, a real life, a real glass of water, real tenderness, real starvation, real harm, psychic real, real geography, utmost real, libidinal social ties, libidinal as in desire, as in lust, hot longing, a hot year, existed earlier, driving force, at the wheel, real motivation, nadir, the currency of titles, the ceremony of polite, nondeterministic political organisation of the psyche, memories tend to the mythical, exterminating angel, prophetic spirit, so completely claimed, seamless, sustaining irony, never restricted the restless, the finitude of philosophical thinking, the banality of political direction, the ingenuity, artistry

iconoclasm, transgressive, transitional truth,
i may yearn, uncertain, interstices,
unresolved contradistinction, from deep
within the struggle of psychic
representation, and social reality, prefigured
division, sudden rupture, fissures clearly
heard, dramatic enigmatic, the narcissistic
myths of negritude, palpable exposures of
the edge of things, of ultimate radiance,
brief pause, dispersed whenever, declivity

where an authentic upheaval can be born,
absolute depersonalisation, hostile to any
attempt to put the individual back where she
belonged,

extremity, the end of the idea, the social antagonism, the phenomenological affirmation of restless urgency, the existentialist evocation of fantasy, the desperate, doomed dialectic of deliverance, audacious, jagged testimony, the defilement of culture, and territory, cut glance, total presence, its displacement, of time, and person, insatiable fear, and desire, psychic trembling, signs, and symptoms, in the silence, intrepid engagements, aggressed by experience, intercut artefact, deadening prose, short

against the leaden, emergent rule,
emergence, estranged naked declivity,
assertion evocation, enigmatic question, the
ambivalence, psychic identification, the
agony, left hand amputation, presence ruins,
primitive, and degenerate, dismembered,
dislocated, epistemic transgression, original,
disturbing, transgressively, demand
desire, they confer civil, innate ethical,
progressive destiny, bent rational, direct
access at this dangerous moment, give proof,
your repentance, the insurrections

show strategy, and tactics, show oneness of origin, revolted fags, the interview ended amicable, an unalterable decision, most extreme, the wild hordes of blacks, her heart sank at the prospect, political treachery, at this dangerous moment, the most extreme forged by circumstance, war, and barbarism achieved, young slaves divinely inspired, armed only with stones, charged bayonets, picks, and hoes, and sticks, armed with language, clutched at horses, pulled off riders, they put mouth around cannon, pulled bullets out of arms, out of canon, swarmed over guns, and gunners, silences nothing, two thousand dead lay upon the field, awaiting restoration, awaiting order, nothing could stop devotion, revolutionary association, temporary equality, broken things, impudent soldiers, lying, and frayed

frayed nerves, exhausted dishonesty, the
most insincere attachment, boundmaster
and slave, these men who had our children,
neither lock nor bolt, neither door, they lived
in opprobrium and dishonour, enter the
villain, idyllic, the destruction, and
convulsion of despair, we lived, and peace,

pretensions of vanity let slip, elegant
drapery, disgusted interruptions, wont to
express, masterly disapproval, celebrated
speech, still clamouring peasants,
property they would not touch, whatever
the status of mother, into historical totality
alienation, constitutive ambivalent,
occlusions, misrecognition, delirium,
neurotic constellation, in accordance,
perverse virtue, avowed ambition, a
formerly fertile caricature, febrile, furtive,
fantasmatic, split presence, distort,
breach, repeats, perverse, bizarrebirth,
palimpsest, transference, fragile

lawlike, figurative condition, black, and
white argument, underlie locus, analytic,
look or locus, external basis, paranoid
fantasy, boundless possession, ascertain,
locus, when glances meet, who does not
dream, fantasmatic, phantasmagorical, no
glances, which permits the dream, splitting
avenge, abandon, tethered deferral,
surrender architecture, disturbing
inbetween, artifice, disposed, disclosing
desire, the question of identification, liminal,
libidinal desire, of look, of language, of limit,
uncertainty dismemberment, no longer
laugh

no longer epidermal, responsible triple
person, in reading, assailed, crumbled,
between intimation psychoanalytic,
domination, sensuous incongruous,
demonic, curious anonymity prototype,
vodou pantheon, loss, ancestor recognised
through dreams, divination, possession, the
machinations of sorcerers, dehuman
menace, undead, squawking loudly, slave
rebel, apathy, zombie, pathological insatiable,
soulless husk, flesh direction,
consolidates, teeming with rebellious, with
impulse of subjugate, of emerge, to find

expression, became a people indigenous to
the site of their struggles, slave whip
sounding, delirium of triumph, rage against
evil fates, raging revolt, born in hills,
nurtured secret, who plotted, and trained,
swooped down upon, in the turns, and
vicissitudes, the underlife had emerged, raging deities,
stranger soil, the africanborn disrupted from
familiar earth, labour expropriated, society
abandoned, in exile from traditions, in letters
of blood, and fire, henceforth the local army,
otherwise things never go weak

impenetrable and stern, excessive aloofness, with the habit and manner of reserve, taught her necessity, selfcontained, lying, deceitful, loquacious mendacity, to be engaged in doing, to sit alongside, reconciliatory, drenched, dying in an alpine prison, to win the only successful slave revolt in history.

FORTHCOMING BY HELA PRESS

SUBMISSION DECLINED
JEFF WALL PRODUCTION

GENDER IS OVER
FILIPKA RUTKOWSKA

RETINA
THÉO CASCIANI